TRUE PAIN

A Real Life Story

By

Kevin Robinson

Acknowledgment

First, I must thank God for sparing my life when I came so close to the point of death. That gift allowed me this opportunity to share my story with you.

I say thank you to the Gleaner Company and Olivia Brown (Journalist with the Gleaner). You saw it fit to interview me that fateful day, and as fate would have it, that interview led to a publishing deal for my book.

Thank you ever so much to my Publishers, Leroy Hutchinson, and Ann- Monique Bailey Hutchinson, along with the O.Y.R. Books and Publishing team.

To all those who supported my vision of writing this book, to my grandmother who has stood by me since birth, thank you for believing in me, and thank you for your prayers.

Table of Contents

Chapter 1

Angry Bullets

The year was 1998. A year that lives with me and one that I can never forget. The events of that year changed my life forever, and they live with me even as I pen this story.

It all started one Sunday evening when two of my friends and I went to look for another of our friends. We always did that when I was not working or on Sunday evenings. It was one of our usual chill spots. We would sit at the roadside, at my friend's gate, and laugh and talk like teenagers tend to do. At that time, none of us knew the promises of that fateful day in December.

Later that December evening, something happened that would change my life forever. From that moment, nothing was ever the same.

In the heights of our innocent conversation and carefree laughter, the horrors of the guns came calling in the evening—horrors which terrify the land of the living and bring forth destruction and death. You could hear the guns as they exalted themselves, echoing near and far. They came to take out one of the world's brightest stars, but my God was right there with me; He was not far. The gunshots screamed in destructive glee, boom! Boom!

Boom, boom! People began to scatter, running in all directions, and that's when I finally tried to escape the horrors of that moment. For a minute, I was running down the road, and the next minute, I found myself on the ground. Reality slowly crawled to my side and painfully kicked me. I noticed that something terrible was wrong with me. I could not move my feet. They shot me. A bullet had punctured my skin and forced its way right through my back. Blood gushed from the wound, and I could feel my skin getting wet as my life in blood raced from my body. I was unable to move, and so I stayed there on the ground, the moist hands of my blood my only company.

It was as if the whole world was getting dark. I felt like I would no longer be a part of this world, but I did not lose consciousness in those horrifying moments. I was still very much aware of my surroundings, but my short life flashed before my eyes. This only worsened when they came. They stood over me and just looked at me. A wicked, vicious, and murderous bunch they were. They fired the shots that wounded me, and then they left me on the ground to die. Silently, they turned their backs to me, to my pain, and walked away. How could they be so heartless? How could they be so cold?

I didn't get to dwell for too long on the reality of their heartlessness. The shooting had subsided. The smoke cleared, and there was a sense of 'calm' — the calm before the storm. People started to come back on the road. For them, nothing had changed, but for me, everything had changed. They finally saw me, forced to lay on the ground in a pool of my blood. They acted quickly and innocently. They took me up and brought me to the main road, a short distance from the lane where I was shot. They soon stopped a passing car —I think it was a private vehicle and not a taxi. They put me inside the car and rushed me to Kingston Public Hospital (KPH). It was as if my mind refused to lose consciousness in those moments. Despite the physical pain of the wound and the mental pain of wondering what the injury meant for my future, I remained awake for the entire journey. When we arrived at the hospital, my good Samaritans lifted me from the car because my legs would not cooperate even then. I can vividly recall when they placed me on a long thing with wheels, which I later found out was called a stretcher.

Many people began to congregate around me as they pushed the stretcher into the famous hospital's emergency area. I am now aware that they were all a part of the medical team, but at that time, they were dressed in different colored clothes and asked me many questions.

"What is your name?" one of them asked.

"My name is Kevin Robinson," I said. I wish I could recall what was going through my mind then.

"Where do you live?" asked another.

I managed to reply with the correct information, "82½ Spanish Town Road, Kingston 13, a place called Boat Island."

The questions continued in quick succession. "Who shot you?" another person asked as the stretcher ride continued.

I told them that gunmen shot me, and that response quickly generated another question. "How old are you?"

"Sixteen," was my brief response.

They then asked for my mother's name, and I told them that my mother's name was Jacqueline Williams and my father's name was George Robinson. By the end of the rushed interview, we were in a room, and seconds later, they placed a huge bright light over my head. They informed me that they would cut my clothes off, which they did. They gave me something to inhale; a wet, soft white piece of cotton with a liquid substance in it. They placed it over my nose and told me to take a deep breath. I inhaled it. Within seconds, my mind finally gave up the struggle, and I lost consciousness. The doctors were left to do their part, and that they did.

Chapter 2

The Hospital-ity

I woke up in bed many hours later. It was a brand-new day and a brand-new life. I was strung up from left to right with a drip in one hand and saline solution in the other. The most devastating realization was the fact that I was now paralyzed from the waist down. Sixteen years of 'ordinary' was all I got, or at least, so I thought in the early stages of my paralysis.

I can recall now how I accessed my new circumstances and physical appearance that day. I had a long cut down the middle of my stomach from where they must have cut me open during surgery the previous night. I had a long tube under my left arm that went through my ribcage and into my stomach. They had taped the tube to my skin to secure it. The tube had a big bottle screwed to the end of it. Based on my observation, it was taking blood from my stomach.

Additionally, a catheter was inserted into my genital and another little tube into the right side of my stomach. On the left side of my stomach, the doctors had cut a place from which I would be able to pass feces. Despite the numerous tubes running in and out of my broken body, another doctor came with an additional tube with a small bag attached. He inserted this tube into my nostril and down into my stomach. It was the most uncomfortable thing that I had ever encountered. I could not eat or drink with the tube.

By that time, the news had spread that I was shot and taken to the Kingston Public Hospital. My brothers, their sister, and their mother visited me while I was at the hospital. I was living with them at the time of the shooting. They were shocked to see the new version of me upon their arrival. They realized that my life had changed, and everything was now upside down. Not only was I shot, but I was also now crippled from the waist down, possibly for the rest of my life. They saw me strung up from left to right, lying on my back, and unable to move. I was only alive because of God's mercy. I was grateful for their visit, but it only made my new reality more devastating.

The next day, my brothers' mother traveled from Kingston. She went to Clarendon, to a place called Sevens Heights, to tell my grandmother, Miss Ruby Brown, the dreaded and unexpected news. I call her granny. She would soon find out that her grandson, Kevin Robinson, was shot by gunmen and newly paralyzed. They spared me the pain of her reaction, and I appreciate that even more today.

After granny had gotten the shocking news, she left Clarendon and came to the hospital to look for me. When I saw my granny coming, I finally wept. I cried because I knew the love she had for me and the love I had for her. I knew then that it hurt her to see me like that. But she was strong, and she still is. Perhaps I inherited some of her strength. She came to my bedside, and we talked; we had a good conversation, but pain and sorrow were dancing to a painfully slow rhythm in my heart. When the hours were spent and visitation time expired, it was time for her to leave. That broke my heart once more, but it was to be my new reality.

This was to be the new normal for many months after that. From that day on, my granny would leave the "country," as we call it in Jamaica, and come to the KPH to visit me every week. She would always reach early in the morning, even long before the doctors checked up on their patients or 'run ward' as we say in Jamaica. She would bring lots of goodies for me, including ripe bananas, oranges, watermelon, and coconut water. Granny carried boiled eggs, soup, and plenty of other niceties for me, and I loved her for her dedication. She also gave me pocket money every time she visited me. My granny, Rubena Brown, my father's mother, is a loving and blessed woman. When I saw no one else, no father or mother, no sister or brother, I could always count on my granny.

So, there I was in the hospital. I was still in shock and disbelief, trying to come to terms with what had happened. I had never been admitted to the hospital. Innocently, I thought to myself, alright then, I will be coming out in a matter of days. But the days slowly turned into weeks. Then the medications started. I would begin to take various pills every day, all of which bore different colors. I took the drug in the morning, at midday, and then at night. I took so many pills that eventually, I could see signs of the passing when I urinated.

Along with the pills, I also got injections every other day. Additionally, I had to do many x-rays during the days and sometimes at night. I had never been in an x-ray room before the shooting and didn't know what to expect. So, when they brought me to the x-ray room, I didn't know inside would have been so chilly. I was shivering the entire time. The porter lifted me from the wheelchair and laid me flat on my back on a long table-like thing. Man, it was so cold. If I could run, I would have, but my feet wouldn't let me. Next, they brought the x-ray machine above me, and I looked straight into it as they completed the process. Afterward, the porter took me back to my bed. This became a regular part of my hospital routine for many weeks.

As the days went by, so did the weeks, and slowly but surely, they turned into months. That's when it hit me; I was going to be in for the long haul. I would not be leaving the hospital any time soon. As I laid on my back, strung up, helpless, and unable to move, a million thoughts crossed my mind.

What if I never walked again? How could this be? Am I dreaming? Is this happening for real? It was real, alright.

The injections and the pain I continued to feel would drag my senses awake and let me know that it was for real. It was all happening. I would eventually begin to tell myself that this is your new reality! You're not dreaming, so stop thinking like that. Even then, I pondered, trying to accept all of it. I thought to myself in resignation, at least nothing else can go wrong. Nothing can get worse.

But boy, oh boy, was I wrong. The porters would turn me now and again, between hours, day, and night because I could not turn myself. One night, I noticed that something was wrong. My skin had begun to peel from my bottom and my hip. They told me that I had something called bedsores because I had spent hours in one position, and the place where I was lying down became hot and sweaty. It was a horrible sight. It was like nothing I ever saw before; I was terrified. I did not believe my own eyes or what I saw. My skin had melted away, leaving large sores. The nurses would dress the wounds and covered them each morning, leaving big, white plasters on my right hip and bottom. After that, a female staff came to bathe me and emptied my urine drainage and colostomy bags with my waste. It was embarrassing. I could not brush my teeth or change myself. I was too weak, and it broke me all over again.

I had lost a lot of blood, and I was in severe pain. Nothing they gave me stopped or even eased the pain temporarily. When I looked at my condition, knowing it was because of another human being's actions, I was devastated. I was a broken man, much like a shattered vessel. It caused me to cry, to see how meager I became in a matter of weeks. My feet had become so slender, like sticks. They continued to take blood from me daily, but I can only recall getting one bag of blood only once.

Furthermore, the tube that went into my stomach also took blood from my stomach for months. I had that tube inserted for so long that I developed an infection in the stomach. That led to another round of treatment, this time at the National Chest Hospital. I had an appointment at the said hospital. My doctor at the KPH sent me to be treated by a specialist for the stomach infection. Each time I visited the doctor there, I traveled by ambulance with a nurse and a porter. I don't recall enjoying any of those rides back and forth.

Dr. Evil…or Not?

One day, I was lying unconcerned in my hospital bed when I felt something fall from my side. I saw that the tube had fallen out as it was only taped to my skin when the doctor inserted it earlier. The tape had gotten wet from sweat and lifted, leaving little support for the tube. It was a good thing I could still use my hands on that day. Instinctively, I covered the area where the tube was previously inserted with my right hand and quickly shouted, "Nurse! Nurse!"

One Nurse ran to me and asked, "What is it, Mr. Robinson?"

I said hurriedly, "mi tube drop out!"

She checked me and acted quickly, using some plaster-like thing to cover it, and then she taped it down. She didn't put the tube back in, but it was a good thing I could use my hand. If I could not use my hand, air would have entered my lungs, and it could have collapsed, possibly resulting in my death. But God was so good to me. I thank God for my hands even today.

After the tube fell out and that situation was sorted out, I thought, well, 'that's that.' I figured everything would stay that way, and all would be well. However, it didn't go that way. My sixteenth year on this earth was full of surprises. To my surprise, the following day, when my doctor came, the nurse had told him what happened. I saw when he went for his toolkit and then came to stand beside me.

The doctor said, "Good morning, Mr. Robinson."

I replied, "Good morning, Doc."

"How are you?" he asked.

"I'm fine," I responded. He put his toolkit on my bed, removed a piece of cotton, and put some liquid on it. He wiped below the area where the tube had fallen from and told me the liquid substance would numb the spot. If only that were the case that morning. That substance did not work at all.

As soon as the doctor started to cut me, I felt every slice the blade made as it unleashed its fury on my flesh. He cut another hole into my side, and blood oozed out like an angry stream. My blood soaked the white sheet on the bed, ruining the sheets and painting it crimson. I cried and screamed as the doctor showed little mercy as he cut into my skin. He was doing his job, and sometimes that requires focus, not mercy. I tried to kick my feet, but they wouldn't obey my mental commands. I took up my pillows and flung them away in agony. Somewhere, even amid the blinding pain, I heard when the nurse asked me, "Mr. Robinson, you don't want your pillow anymore?"

I did not answer her. I could not answer her. How could she ask such a thing when I was in so much pain?

When the doctor finished cutting into my skin, he took up another bottle with a tube. He reached into his toolkit and removed a scissors-like tool. He pushed it into the hole he had just created in my tortured body, seemingly to lift one of my ribs, and then inserted the tube. As he did so, I could feel my blood streaming down my side. He made no mistake this time. He put his needle and thread to work and stitched the tube into place. Once again, I felt the wrath of the needle as it stung my flesh, making its presence felt as I twisted and turned in agony.

Finally, the doctor finished and left my bedside. The torture was over, and my mind and body could finally begin to recover from the necessary assault. A nurse came and changed the blood-soaked sheets and my clothes. She bathed me shortly after that. To my surprise, as I would later discover, during that horrific moment, my granny had come to visit me.

She was there, watching the entire painful process. She saw everything. I wish she hadn't, but it was beyond my control. One of the nurses went to her, and as she led her away, she said, "come, grandma." She returned shortly and completed her responsibilities towards me. At that point, the nurse brought back my grandmother. I saw the sadness on her face as she walked towards me, and I knew it was because of what she saw. Despite this, she still came over to my bed, and we talked. She gave me goodies as usual and my pocket money. We were there until it was time for her to leave. Every time she turned and walked away, I remember feeling sad because I wished I could go with her. I loved my granny so much that when it was time for her to leave, I left like she took a piece of me with her.

Mentally Sound

Time crept by, and there I was, lying in the hospital bed day after day and night after night. That was when life presented its most significant challenges to my mental state of being. Paralysis put my mind to the greatest test yet. How would I manage this reality that I am now left to face, I wondered? How would I cope? How would I adapt to changes, like not being at home and not sleeping in my bed? I knew changes like not having my friends around all the time, not working, and not going to the game shop to play games anymore were imminent. Never again would I have the chance to play football, my favorite sport. I would never be able to go to the river again or shoot birds with my friends. I would not be able to have a shower by myself. I was devastated, and I knew it was not about to get better anytime soon. That reality was scary, but so were the realities of the other patients in the hospital.

Amid my painful journey, I saw things I never saw before on a scarily regular basis. I saw people in bandages, wounded and covered in blood or dying, all around me. One night, a guy came in with gunshot wounds, I think. They inserted a tube in his nose, like the one they inserted in mine. With that tube, you could neither eat nor drink. Later that night, he disobeyed the doctor's orders, and it was a fatal mistake that he paid for with his life. He left the bed, went to the pipe, and drank water with the tube still in his nose. He didn't live for ten minutes after. I vividly recall the moment I saw the Nurse draw the partition between our beds, and the porter wrapped him in a white sheet, placed him on a stretcher, and took him away. He was stiff-stone-dead.

Police officers were up and down, in and out of the hospital daily. Sometimes, they brought prisoners in handcuffs for various reasons. If they were to spend the night there, the police would cuff one of their hands to the bedhead. The prisoners had to sleep that way. Life was happening all around me, but nothing could change my new reality of paralysis.

Chapter 3

Country Life

L ife does not happen according to our will. My mother, Jacqueline Williams, had to learn this lesson very early. She was sixteen years old when the principal discovered that she was pregnant. She didn't know she was pregnant, but she carried me all the way. She was impregnated against her will. Someone introduced her to the idea of abortion, but she closed the door on that possibility. Despite her struggles at home, where she was severely mistreated, most persons encouraged her to keep the baby, so she pushed through.

I was told that when I was born, her circumstances became even more difficult. She lived with her mother and her mother's husband. He made my mother uncomfortable, and their relationship was tense. As a result, she had to leave her home with nowhere to go.

She spent nights on the street and, in some cases, crept into people's kitchens if she knew them so she could have a place to sleep with her baby. She had to wait until they were asleep before she made her move.

People said I would cry a lot, and she would often feed me with breast milk to stop my cries even though she was also hungry and without food. Out of desperation, she had to give me water to drink from the buckets other persons used to store water to flush their toilets.

She was a young single mother, unemployed and inexperienced. She decided to go to the "country" and asked my father's mother, Granny, to keep me for a while so she could find a job to take care of me. I was ten months old when she left and went back to Kingston. She wrote letters to Granny to check on me, and she would often send 'things' for me. This helped my grandmother, and my mother reportedly visited me on occasions.

I can't recall anything about my mother before I was about seven or eight years old. I was told everything I know about her before then, but I remember when she returned to the country for me. When she arrived at my grandmother's house, she introduced herself to me. She told me she would ask Granny if she could take me back to her home for some quality time. Strangely, she felt the need to ask my grandmother for permission, but Granny did not stop her.

She took me to her house, where I discovered that she had another child, a little girl, by then. I now had a younger sister. Being at my mother's house was strange for me. I didn't stay there for a long time. After the school holiday ended, I went back to be with Granny.

Growing up with Granny was fun for me. I lived with her, her husband, and my cousin. Granny's husband was like a father to me. He showed me a lot of love, and he also taught me discipline. Some things were taken from my life, but they are always replaced by something just as good or even better in one way or the other.

Every morning, I woke up early, prayed, and then made my bed. We ate breakfast outside, cleaned the house, polished the floors, and did other household chores. I would also feed the cows and fowls, take the goats to the bushes, harvest eggs, and more before leaving for school.

I am not from a financially wealthy background, but my memories of the past, many of them, are rich with moments of peace and uninhibited happiness. I would have to cut one pencil into two for school, but I didn't mind.

On the first day of basic school, I cried. I said to Granny, "mi nuh wah gah school, mi wah tan a yard."

This quickly became a song that other children sang when they saw me. I didn't take long to get comfortable in school, though, and soon enough, basic school became fun for me. My teacher was nice, and I was able to play a lot. Granny would pick me up from school, although I could find my way home.

My grandmother was a strict Christian woman. Going to Church and Sunday school was compulsory for me. After Sunday school, I would have to tell my grandmother what I learned, and I would have to recite the golden text. I didn't mind this either because Sunday school was fun. It was even more fun knowing that I would go home to a lovely meal because Granny was an excellent cook. She is restricted now from doing what she could do then, but I recall the beauty of those moments very well.

The clothes we wore to Church back then were unusual. Some of the pants would have one pocket, either at the front or the back and were made from pepper seed material. Sometimes, the pants had no pocket at all. The shoes were extremely pointy in the toe area. I found both the shoes and clothing to be embarrassing to wear at times.

There was no electricity in my community at the time. We used a kerosene oil lamp and bottle torch instead. Sometimes, I had to travel far to find wood for fires for cooking purposes especially. There was no piped water which meant that I would have to ride a donkey cart one mile to get water. The donkey's name was Margaret, and she was very faithful. Sometimes the wheel would fall off the cart, and other times, the steering would fall from the socket, causing the containers to fall from the cart with the water. Sometimes, they would be damaged, and my cousin and I suffered bruises, but it was all fun and games for me. I was having the time of my life.

My childhood was action-packed. Granny would plant gungo, a type of pea, a variety of beans, cassava, yam, sweet potato, and other ground provisions. I was surrounded by trees in the yard and community, including mango, grapefruit, orange, lime trees. I would help with farming – removing stones and weeds and planting seeds. My grandmother previously worked in tobacco and cane fields, so she was used to the hard work. At times, I could not manage the farm work, but I pushed as hard as possible for my Granny's sake.

When I got the chance to do it, I would also shoot birds with my friends, and at other times, I walked for more than a mile to go to the mango bush, where I would enjoy eating mangoes until I was full. I would also use it as another opportunity to shoot birds. I competed with my friends to see who could shoot the most birds. I may have won a few of those competitions, but for the numerous wasp bites I often endured

When I wasn't out shooting birds, I would often go to the river with my friends to bathe and catch shrimp. Sometimes we would spend the entire day at the river, and when I returned home, Granny would give me dinner and send me to get ready for bed. It didn't end there, however. Granny would take a strap to me, beating me for my long absences. Sometimes, my grandmother's husband would be responsible for administering the discipline. One of his feet was amputated, but even so, he was able to hold me when he thought I needed a beating. He used a strap called "Tan Tuddy" to beat me. I survived their version of discipline without any significant event.

My friends and I often played marbles, and on numerous occasions, we would also make gigs and compete. Clean and fun competition. Nothing beats the skateboards my friends and I made and rode around on. The fresh wind blowing around us as we skated was exhilarating, and because of that, I didn't mind too much that we would often have to travel far to go to the shop.

School days

When I graduated from basic school, my parents were not present. It made my heart heavy when I watched the other children with their parents. I remember the feeling of loneliness that engulfed me as a child. Thankfully, I was not lonely for long because Granny was there for me every step of the way, loving and supporting me, which brought me comfort.

When I was about to start primary school, my grandmother bought me new clothes, shoes, and a bag to go to school. On the first day of school, Granny dressed me neatly and sent me off to school right after breakfast. The morning routine involved my grandmother making breakfast and lunch for me, and the latter she would pack and give me for school. As I got older, I stopped taking lunch as often, and instead, I began to take lunch money to purchase my lunch during the day.

Kevin the Businessman

I started selling various items when I was eleven years old. I did this until I was fifteen years old. I would sell on

Fridays and Saturdays to make some extra money. Soon enough, I would gamble away all the money and lose it all. When I got home, my grandmother would punish me, but I did not doubt her love for me even then. There was more to come for me. When Granny found out I was gambling, she made a man beat me out by the shop where I used to gamble. It was a beating I will never forget, but it came with some solid advice during and after the beating. The man advised me to stay away from gambling. He told me that gambling was not a hobby in which I should partake.

Sometimes, I would go to the theatre to watch movies, which made me get home late.

I was an industrious young man, and as much as I wanted to have fun, I wanted to make money as well. I would sell at the market and push handcarts to carry luggage for persons to make extra money. I would also help persons carry their groceries at the supermarket.

When the Christmas season drew near, I would be busy working and earning monies in multiple ways on Christmas Eve and Boxing Day. Grand Market was a big deal for me; that is where I would make most of my money. Christmas in the country was the best. It was exciting, cool, and everything a young boy wanted at the time. The food was terrific, and Granny cooked a feast every Christmas. I was responsible for getting the ice, so I had to travel to purchase it because there was no electricity in our community. Granny did not have a refrigerator at the time because of this.

Neighbors would visit each other's houses in the Christmas season to celebrate and share food and more. I enjoyed those holidays more than anything else.

My grandmother raised me to have manners and respect. I had to greet each adult and visitor when they came around, and I could not use explicit language in their presence. Otherwise, they would tell Granny about what I did or did not do.

On New Year's Eve, I would go to Church with Granny for Watch night service until after midnight. This was the tradition then, and in some places, it still is. I didn't mind this as a child. My life taught me so much then and continues to be my biggest teacher even now.

Father and Son

I am one of seven children (all boys) for my father. My father lived in Kingston for as long as I can recall, but one day, many years ago, my grandmother allowed me to travel from Clarendon to visit my father. The experience was strange for me. It was new and completely different from living in the country. I watched a lot of television while visiting with my father because I now had access to cable television. My brother took me around the area to introduce me to everyone, and persons gave me the nicknames "Reds" and "Country man." I didn't mind the names. I was too young to care about certain things, and even now, life is too precious to care about certain things.

While I stayed with my father, I helped my brother's mother to sell at her stall. At one point, I went to the coronation market in downtown Kingston to purchase thyme for resale. After selling for some time, I obtained a job at a cook shop close to where I lived. I did all of this while I was still attending school. Maybe this caused my struggle with reading at the time. Who knows, but it certainly caused the powers that be to put me in a lower grade. I was an active youth, and I enjoyed every minute of these early years. Well, most of it.

Tragedy struck for the first time in my life. No, it wasn't my time yet, but it was a painful period in my life. One day, my brother's friend called him out of my father's house to accompany him to a particular location. I was at my new school in Kingston at that time, and while I was there, I noticed that a friend of mine, a little girl, was absent. I didn't think much about it. When I heard a series of bullets barking nearby, I didn't think much of it either. The sound of gunshots was no stranger to me at the time.

The class went to recess shortly after, and I went to sit on the front steps of my school. I looked up when I saw someone approaching me soon after I sat down. I quickly recognized that it was my little friend, the girl who was absent from class earlier. She was crying, and as she drew closer, I called out to her and asked her why she was crying.

In her innocence, she stated, "Yuh brother dead. Dem shot him and kill him."

I was shocked. I did not know that the bullets I heard earlier were ending my brother's life. I jumped to my feet, rushed back into the class, grabbed my bag, and walked out of school. I was in a daze, but I made it home. I didn't know what to do at the time, and no one else was home. I laid down quietly, and somehow, I fell asleep.

When I woke up, I was no longer alone, and the details of my brother's fatal walk slowly came to life.

My brother had followed his friend to an area reasonably close to our home and my school. One more of his friends arrived shortly after, and after a brief conversation, this friend pulled a gun and shot my brother. The bullets ended my brother's life immediately, severing his head from his body. The brutal execution of my brother was my first experience with tragedy in Kingston. He was only a few years over thirty years old. Life was never quite the same after that day; nothing is after tragedy travels through a family.

Chapter 4

The Strength of a "Granny"

A t the age of sixteen, my new circumstances were very hard for me. Gunshot wounds or paralysis are not things sixteen-year-olds expected at that time in history. Perhaps today, with the country's current crime problems but back then, it was a shock to the system. I couldn't find words to describe how I felt; it's like time stood still, but I couldn't stand.

I felt like I lost my purpose, and I couldn't find my will to fight. But during all that, I would eventually identify a steady point of hope. It was my granny, Ruby Brown. Knowing that she was there for me and would always visit me weekly reminded me that I was not alone and that someone cared for me.

That gave me hope. She was like the wind beneath my broken wings and my tower of strength. I am one of those Jamaicans who can genuinely speak to the blessing of a faithful grandparent and the importance of their presence in a child's life. My mother was not present at that time, and neither was my father. Still, my grandmother ably filled their shoes without hesitation, with love and gentle patience. The strength of my grandmother was my strength then and remains so today.

Far from Home

By then, I met some wonderful people, including both nurses and patients. One day, two doctors stood close to my bed while having a conversation and looking at me. I thought I overheard one say that he was going to send me home. Upon hearing what I thought I heard, tears came to my eyes. I missed my home and so badly wanted to go home. I felt happy, but it would not last for long. To my surprise, I heard wrongly. I wasn't going home at all. What the doctor had said was that they would be sending me to Hope Mona Rehab. It was the beginning of another hospital stay, but this time, it was specifically for people with disabilities. They were sending me there to see if I had a chance of walking again—a small glimmer of hope. Could it be? Did I have a chance at an unhindered life after all? Only time would tell.

I must say, though, that it wasn't so bad being at the KPH. The doctors and nurses treated me well despite my frequent calls to them when I was in pain. I was a child, and at times, the pain was unbearable. I had no choice. Sometimes, it felt like my heart hurt because of the pain I felt due to my injuries. The cut I got in the center of my belly, where the doctors had cut me open that day of the shooting, wasn't stitched. They only dressed it and left it to heal. As a result of the severe pains, the cut healed with many wrinkles. I tended to flex or tense my body whenever the pain would become unbearable, contributing to the incision's uneven healing. Nothing the doctors gave me eased the pain. That's how intense it was, overwhelmingly so.

Eventually, the time came for them to transfer me to the Mona Rehabilitation Center. They told my granny, so she arrived early that morning. The Nurse changed my bandages, bathed, and clothed me. They had already packed all my personal belongings. It was time for me to go.

Leaving the KPH to go to another hospital rather than to my home was heartbreaking. It made me sad for many reasons, but most significantly, I had been there for about six months and met some charming people. I had to leave them and those memories behind. I was going to a new hospital where I knew no one and would have to start all over again.

It was time. The porter lifted me from the bed and into the wheelchair with which I was quickly becoming familiar. I was ready to go, but as the porter slowly pushed the wheelchair away, I waved goodbye to my old friends. A sadness slowly creeping through me as he led me away, turned the corner, and headed towards the elevator. Upon reaching the elevator, the porter opened the door for us to enter. Aside from granny and the porter, a nurse was with me as we left. The porter pressed the button, closing the door to my stay at the KPH and locking us into the silence of the elevator ride.

The Road to Recovery

You could hear a pin drop as the elevator hurried its way silently downstairs. After a couple of minutes, it finally came to a stop. The porter opened the door, and we all exited out and headed towards the location where the ambulance waited. As we stood beside the ambulance, the porter opened the ambulance door and pressed a button. Slowly, something like a lift came down, and I knew it was for my use. I rolled the wheelchair onto it, and it took me straight up into the ambulance. Granny, the nurse, and the porter came inside after that, and the porter closed the door. Everyone settled in their seats. The driver started the engine, and away we went, off to another place where I knew not.

After driving for some time, we finally reached the Mona Rehab. The security guard at the gate approached the ambulance and made some checks. He soon opened the gate, and the ambulance drove in until it came to a stop. The porter assisted me from the ambulance and down the lift. The other occupants of the ambulance accompanied us over to the section of the hospital where they registered me. Afterward, I was admitted to the ward. Once more, the porter came to my rescue, putting me into what would become my bed for the next few weeks. They unpacked my belongings and put them away. The nurse and porter left with the ambulance, by my grandmother stayed for a while. She familiarised herself with the new hospital where she would now come to visit me. It was a much longer journey than the one she was accustomed to taking when I was at the KPH, but I knew then that she would make the sacrifice for me.

So, there I was at this new hospital, where I knew no one, and there stood my granny, once more by my bedside. She was always a constant in my life. I am not sure where I would be if she hadn't decided to love me the best way she knew how. We chatted for a little while, looked around, and hailed other patients and people around us. I may have inherited her friendly mannerism. The time soon came for granny to leave. It was another sad moment for me, but I knew that she had to go. This was yet another reality to which my new life forced me to adapt.

If I were to survive at my location, my only option was to start making friends right away. Somehow, I knew by then that I would not be going home anytime soon, and so, it made sense that I try to make myself comfortable. I am a humble guy and a people person, so I didn't have any difficulty making friends. Before long, on that first day of my arrival, I was making new friends. It worked like a charm; I was chatting and laughing already with nurses and patients. They saw the gloom of sadness on my face after my granny left the hospital, and so my new friends tried to cheer me up as best as possible. It is not strange that I felt that way at the time. She is my granny. She raised me from I was a young ten-month-old baby boy, and when I needed her the most, she was there for me. So, you see, we shared a powerful bond. She is like my mother, my father, my sister, and my brother all in one. She is my everything, a whole part of me. I could always bet my life on her coming to visit me every weekend while I was in the hospital. When I saw no one else, I could always count on my granny to be there for me. She was like my winning trump card, my lucky coin, a sure bet.

Sometime later that evening, one of the nurses came over to me, pushing a little kart with various items on it. She told me to roll up my sleeve, and I did. She wrapped the sphygmomanometer around my arm to check my blood pressure and found it to be normal. She followed up by checking my temperature. I told her that I had bed sores: one on my right hip and the other on my bottom. Now that I think about it, she would have already known this. She had a docket containing all my medical information by then. She did all her checks, talked with me a little, and left shortly after. After that, a short, distinguished-looking man dressed in a white shirt and dark pants came to my bedside. With a stethoscope around his neck, he introduced himself as my doctor, Doctor Griffith.

I said quietly, "Nice to meet you, Doc. My name is Kevin Robinson."

He talked with me, took a small light from his shirt pocket, and pointed it at me while looking into my eyes.

He then took the stethoscope from around his neck, placed it on my stomach, and listened intently to my heartbeat. He then set the instrument on my back and, once more, listened carefully. Before he left my bedside, he examined the location of the injuries I now sported because of my inability to move. He left shortly after that.

As I rested in the bed, I could finally take in everything around me. As I did so, I keenly observed some amazing sights. I saw situations I never saw before, including patients with multiple disabilities. My mind filled with wonder; I continued to look around unblinkingly. I saw gunshot victims like myself who were left paralyzed for life. There were also accident victims who were disabled for the rest of their life. Some of the patients could not use their hands to do anything. They couldn't feed themselves. Others couldn't turn on their own, so someone had to assist them. Someone had to do everything for them.

But hang on, there is more. Some were born with various deformities; some were disabled from birth; others never got the chance to walk. Some couldn't talk properly and could only wink their eyes and turn their heads. Others had their hands turned inside out, while a few patients had portions of their limbs amputated. I never saw anything like that; it was a shocking sight. I saw how well the nurses and everyone interacted with the patients. They treated them with so much care; you could see and feel the love. In my mind, I thought that no matter the position you're in, whether you were born that way or otherwise, you are unique, and you are worthy of being loved.

As time passed, I was up and about in a wheelchair riding around the compound, viewing the place, and getting to know different people. I met some very nice, loving, and caring people that genuinely looked out for persons with disabilities.

In the morning, bathing time was about 4:30 am to 5:00 am. Those who could go to the bathroom would go, but someone would bathe us and comb our hair if necessary, for those who could not do so on their own. They would also empty our catheters and change our pampers. After that, they made our beds, making sure that we smelled fresh, nice, and clean. They would then turn their attention to dressing those who had bedsores. After some time, Doctors would come to 'run ward,' meaning each doctor would check on their patient.

One morning, my doctor came to my bedside, pulled back the bandages from the bedsores, and inspected them closely. He didn't stay long after that. Instead, he left my bedside to attend to other patients nearby. After he had finished "running ward," he returned to my bed with a toolkit in his hand. He placed it on the bed, opened it, and pulled back the bandages covering bedsores on my bottom. He took out a piece of medical cotton, soaked it with a liquid I could not identify and wiped the sore area. Next, he reached into his toolkit and took out a tiny shiny object looking like a small knife.

I was watching his every move. I was not anticipating what would come because of that cutting instrument. He started to cut into the location of the bedsore, continuing for about half an hour or so. He said that dead flesh was forming at the site, so he had to cut them out for new flesh to grow. His hand, which held the cutting tool, showed no mercy. I cried. I cried like a baby. I think I almost passed out from crying as much as I did, and the pain I felt as the knife sliced deeper and deeper into my flesh. It unleashed its fury, severing my flesh piece-by-piece. The bed was soaked with my blood as if I was having a blood bath. In my young mind, it was like a scene from a horror film. Finally, he finished addressing the wound with the metal tool, dressed it, closed his toolkit, and left someone in charge of taking off the blood-soaked sheets and bathing me. At the time, I wondered if he would ever stop. That day is not the type of day I recall fondly but let us continue with the trip down memory lane.

Chapter 5

I Tried

A change was coming, or so I hoped. Physiotherapy was set to begin. The usual morning routine of waking up, getting my wounds dressed, showering then having breakfast was about to change. I didn't mind the routine, mainly because a part of it meant I had time to chat with other patients at the rehabilitation center. Sometimes, I would do this all day, stay in bed, chat, socialize, make new friends, or get to know my new friends better. And then it was time to hit the gym. I was excited because a part of me knew this could mean something good for my legs and the ability to use them again. So, when it was time to get physiotherapy in the gym, I was not scared. I was hopeful. The physical therapists wanted to see if there was anything they could do to help me walk again. This included doing specific exercises regularly. I went to the gym about three days a week, and while I was there, I was engaged with lifting weights, some heavier than others. The therapists did several exercises with my feet. This included using the drop foot brace, which was designed to help the weakened foot so that the user can exercise.

They also had shoes specially made for people in my condition. During the exercises, the therapists would put these shoes on me and stretch my legs. They would then wrap what looked like a batsman's pad on each of my legs, put a long, straight piece of board behind the pad, and then used a sprain strap to wrap them on each foot. Then they would put me to stand upright, between two long, horizontal iron bars. I would use my two hands to hold onto the bars for support while I stood to prevent myself from falling. And with that, I could move up and down between the bars. Just like that, I could feel what it was like to stand on my feet again. Although the various mechanisms greatly assisted me, I stood and looked tall for a little while. It was exhilarating. Then they would remove the pads, the boards, and the wraps. Once again, I was back to my new restricted reality. It was almost like going back from 100 all the way down to zero.

During another series of exercises, the therapists would let me lay on my belly on a bed or a mat. They would then tape some fine wires, with little flat square-shaped ends, on my back, and these would give off a tingling shock. I think they may have been called electromyographs. I could be wrong, but the therapists tried to bring back the damaged nerves by applying little electrical shock waves to them, and it was working! After going to the gym and especially after this treatment, I remember the tingling feeling of active nerves in my feet, especially when I tried to move my toes. I felt this in my feet before, but the sensation became more robust with the targeted exercises. These types of activities continued each time I went to the gym.

Painfully though, despite the length of time, I was there for, there was still no sign of me walking again. But every day, my hope would grow, and my faith would lift higher with my high hope. Maybe, just maybe, one day, I would walk again. At least, this is what a part of me wanted to believe but, when I looked at my feet and saw how meager or, as we say in Jamaica, "mawga" they were, reality began to sink in just a little more. A million thoughts began to rush through my mind, flooding me with apparent fear and a billion questions. What if I never walk? How would I manage? What am I going to do? These were only a few of the questions I had to ask myself, but I didn't have any answers at that time.

When they turned off the lights at night, all kinds of thoughts would hit me like a tornado. They played on my mind as if they were taunting me. I could see them so clearly as if they were standing before me. At nights more than any other time, I went to the world in my head, and there, it was like time stood still, and I was spinning, twisting, and turning, wondering what was going on. I was struggling to accept what my reality was forcing me to acknowledge. In that private world, I wondered, is this all a big misunderstanding? Am I in a dream? Maybe in the morning, when I awoke, everything would be back to normal. I thought this, and I hoped my thought would become my life.

But every morning, I woke and looked at myself; it was not a dream. It was my reality, staring me right in my face, telling me, "this is real, and you will have to accept it. From now on, this is how your life is going to be." Reality's voice was a cold, life-changing voice. Believe me, when I really, and truly paused, and looked at the reality that I had to face, tears fell from my bewildered eyes. There was no way of getting around it or fixing the situation. I was emotionally drained and mentally exhausted because of the restless hours that would unravel my mind nightly and revealed, almost with glee, my troubled soul.

Even as I dealt with my new physical reality, memories of my past flooded my wary and aching mind. All my childhood days were flashing so quickly before me like a subway station on a busy working day — the good times, the not-so-good times, and the bad times. All of these taunted me. Life left me two choices: hang on to the past's good times or deal with the present. I made a choice. I chose the present. Why was this, considering all the pain that the present now had to offer? The good times of the past couldn't help me now. If anything, holding on to the past was what was preventing them from moving forward.

So, I started to embrace the now, the new me that I had become. Firstly, I began to learn how to help myself, which in my case, was vital. I didn't want to put a strain on or be a burden to anyone. I started to learn to bathe myself in bed. I couldn't reach all my body because my feet were very long. I am a tall guy. So, I would ask someone to wash my feet for me. I would comb my hair, put on my shirt, and have someone put on my underpants. A chain hung over my bed from the ceiling, and a wheelchair was always at my bedside. These were all placed there for my convenience based on my limitations.

Whenever I wanted to go for a ride around the center, I would hold the chain and swing myself off the bed and into the chair. Comfortably seated in my own ride, I would travel to the gym or the JAMAL classes available for patients at the rehabilitation center. JAMAL is the abbreviation we use to refer to the Jamaica Foundation for Lifelong Learning. This institution was a training school to which we were given special access at the time. I will always be grateful for the time I spent at JAMAL.

I had fallen way behind when it came to reading, so I would attend these classes to learn and sharpen my mind. The truth was, I wasn't an excellent reader, although I had graduated from the ninth grade. This mishap would not prevent me from trying, in any case. If disabilities could not dictate to me, why should the current state of my brain? Our minds can be trained, after all. And so, the instructors would also teach me to do barbering. They were trying to teach me and others at least one skill. Teaching me this skill gave me a tool, so I still had a sense of independence despite my physical challenges. This skill increased my chances of survival in a world where limitations were not necessarily readily accepted. I started by cutting other patient's hair. I was no expert, but I was doing my thing. Of course, I wasn't getting paid for these haircuts; they were voluntary work. The important thing was, I learned how to cut hair.

Additionally, I was gifted with my own shears and scissors; it was a good feeling. Even amid my pain, I was still growing. I had to do this if I had any intention of regaining lasting joy or peace of mind.

Chapter 6

I'm out of Here

I was at the Mona Rehab for about five months and a few weeks. I spent months in the gym, hours exercising, but no matter how hard the therapists tried, my legs remained unkind to them and me. There was simply nothing coming from my legs. The therapists tried everything, gave their best, but nothing happened for me in that area. We all concluded that my walking days were over for good as far as it was within our power.

One day, one of the nurses came to me, and she said gently, "Mr. Robinson, you are about to be discharged. You will be going home."

Of course, when I heard that, a mixture of emotions coursed through my mind at the time. It was good news on the one hand, but on the other hand, it was horrible news. Once again, I would be leaving all the wonderful, loving, and kind-hearted people I met in that season of my life. They had become like family to me, and now, I had to leave them all behind once again. I would miss them dearly. Ironically, it was like the days could not wait for me to go home because, like clockwork, they were ticking away in rapid succession. Finally, the day and time came for me to go home.

My family, with whom I would be living, was already notified of my intended return home, and they came for me with a taxi. For me, returning home going was a strange feeling both mentally and physically.

Physically, I looked different. I was very skinny. My skin was looking pale, almost white. My feet were so meager and small, and my knees had nearly turned backward, if you get the picture. I may have to wear a catheter at my side for the rest of my life, or I would have to urinate in a bottle forever. Someone would have to assist me whenever I had to take a bath. Someone would have to change my clothes and my sheets. I was accustomed to doing some of these things in the hospital, but the setup was not the same at my home. It was almost as if I would have to relearn these things in a new space.

Mentally, all these things were just playing on my mind. How would my family react when they see me? How would they adjust to the new me that was coming home? When my friends looked at me, what would they think? These thoughts were just taunting me as I made my way home. The change was coming at me once more, and without a doubt, I would have to deal with it as it came.

Home at Last

Before you knew it, the taxi drove up to the lane where I lived before all the drama. As the car slowly turned left into the lane, I crouched down into the backseat because I didn't want anyone to see me. The taxi slowly drove through the lane with the tinted back windows wounded all the way up. The car continued further along the way and made another left turn before it came to a stop at my gate.

Then someone came out to us, opened the gate and the car door, and lifted me out of the car. I was taken inside the house and put me on a bed. They also brought in my stuff from the car, and just like that, I was home at last. Wow. The feeling was strange, but it also felt good. I'd been away from home for so long, almost a year. Anyway, family members who were present when I came home, and other people in the yard, came inside to find out how I felt. As the days went by, word started to go around that I had returned home. The community people were coming to look for me along with some of my fake friends, whom I thought were real. I agree now more than ever with the old proverb, "if you want to know your true friends, form drunk when you see them coming and lay on the roadside, and then you will truly know who your real friends are." I was in the hospital for about one year, from December 1998 to December 1999, and only two of my friends came to look for me. They came once. Not even my former boss, who I worked for at the little restaurant I mentioned earlier, came to visit me in the hospital.

My big brother came, bathed me in the mornings, and changed my dressings before he went to work. I only allowed him to look after me. I didn't let anyone else see me without my clothes because I was ashamed of myself. I was embarrassed to be in this state. When it was bathing or dressing time, everyone had to leave the house, and my brother shut the door. They would only come back inside when he was finished helping me. I would then have some breakfast, and after that, I spent the rest of the day in bed watching TV and talking with family and friends.

My granny would still leave the country every week and come to look for me. She also brought some goodies for me, including coconut water, ripe bananas, oranges, soup, boiled eggs, and roots. She would do her best for me, just to make me feel comfortable. I was still staying with my brother's mother because that's where I was living when I got shot. They treated me very well. They made sure that I was well-fed, never hungry, always clean, my clothes were washed, and smelling fresh. My brother's sister, Kareen, was the one who would wash my clothes. She would wash for me almost every day.

When I just came out of the hospital, I was weak, so sometimes, I would either urinate or defecate in my clothing. On other occasions, I did both simultaneously. This made it necessary for her to wash my clothes daily, and she did this even though she had a young baby at the time. I appreciated the sacrifice then and now. She didn't have to do it, but she chose to help me, and she did it well.

Into the Out

Day after day, I would lay there in my bed, too reluctant to leave the house. Then one day, I decided to go outside. I asked someone to lift me and put me into the wheelchair, and they did so. Shortly after that, I wheeled myself from my bedroom, and finally, there I was for the first time in the yard riding my wheelchair. I don't know what got to my head shortly after I went outside, but I decided that I would "buss a stunt." I rocked back the chair, tilting it on the two back wheels with the front wheels hoisted up in the air. I was stunting, and it felt good! This was only until the chair tilted over backward with my two feet hanging in the air. The sound of feet running in my direction was evident, and then I felt someone taking me up. Fortunately, the fall didn't hurt any part of me, but it was a good laugh. I laughed until I nearly cried because I thought it was funny. Since that time, I have not attempted any more stunts. I left it alone. That thing was not for me.

After the fall, I went for a ride, a much different ride this time around. I went out into the lane. I didn't stay for long because I did not want too many people to see me. I was back home very quickly. The reality was that you could hear gunshots, near or far, at the time, day, and night. Since I didn't have the luxury of obedient feet to run away from another shooting, the inside of my yard was the best place for me. My friends passed through now and again, and some asked if I knew the persons who shot me. But I could tell them nothing because I didn't see their faces. I was face down on the ground when the shooting happened in 1998. Maybe if I knew who it was, I wouldn't have told my friends anyway because I would not want anyone's blood on my hands. I say this because I knew what would have taken place even at that age if I did. It would be certain death but not for my friends or me. On the other hand, someone would have had to pay for what they had done to me. If that happened, then whoever took revenge on my behalf would leave me feeling guilty because of the death of those persons.

My friends were mad at whoever shot me because I didn't do anyone any harm, and they messed me up very badly. So, there could have been retaliation, the consequences of which would have been devastating. I don't think that I could live with myself in those circumstances. So eventually, they stopped asking because I had nothing to tell. That's how life is. People lose interest eventually, especially when information sharing is limited. I didn't mind. I didn't know the shooters, and that, in many ways, made healing easier.

Chapter 7

From Town to Country

In the daytime, I was never bored. I would watch TV all day, including cable, movies, wrestling, and cartoons. I enjoyed watching cartoons. Also, there were always people around to talk with, be it family members or other persons. The yard was a big family yard with about four houses. The adults would gamble during the daytime, playing bingo or card, and so people were constantly coming and going. Even though I was in bed most of the time, I would sometimes go and participate in the bingo games, and sometimes, I even won a game or two.

One weekend, when granny came to look for me, she said, "Kevin, I am going to take you down the country with me so that I can look after you better and give you much closer attention."

Of course, this was good news for me. I would live with granny again, and I knew that I would get the best treatment. My grandmother spoiled me on a whole other level. But at the same time, I said to myself that, "Yeah, granny, I am going to come but not yet."

I started to think about all the beautiful, sexy, half-naked women that I'd be leaving behind. The women who lived in the yard and those who came to gamble were sometimes scantily clad, and you could see a little bit too much. To be honest, I loved looking up their avenue. Ha, what can I say? I am a man, and I love women.

There was this girl who would enter the house to dry off whenever she took a bath. Usually, she stood right in front of me, removed her towel, dried off, and then lotioned herself. It was like my eyes were under a spell as I watched. She didn't seem to care that I was there...and so I thought she might have liked me, but she never told me this. She often assisted me with breakfast or dinner. During the day, if I told her that I needed something to eat, she would buy something for me, even if it meant using money which she had to purchase other necessary items. She also made soup for me on several occasions.

So, when Granny told me that she would take me back to the country, I was like, "Am not ready!"

But my father was there. He shouted, or roared, whichever works, as if he were a lion, "Now!" When he said now, he meant now. The argument was done. Case closed. I lost, and he won. So, they started to pack my stuff for the relocation. Before I knew it, it was time for me to go. I shed a few tears and said my goodbyes. With all my stuff in the car, my father came inside the house, lifted me out of bed, put me in the car's front seat, and shut the door. Granny was already in the car when my father did this. My father entered the driver's seat, closed his door, started the engine, and drove out of the lane. We were off.

As the car drove further away, the city became smaller and smaller as I watched through the rare view mirror. Soon enough, Kingston faded out of sight, and I knew that I wouldn't pass this way again. We drove for what seemed like forever, and finally, we arrived in the parish of Clarendon. We approached Sevens Heights, the district where I was from originally. When the car turned into the community, I wound up the tinted window, much like I did when heading back home from Mona Rehab in Kingston. I didn't want anyone to see me because I didn't leave here in this state. I didn't even want anyone to see me exiting the car. As I peeked out, I realized that the coast was clear. Thank goodness no one was on the road, I thought to myself.

When the car finally came to a stop at granny's gate, I looked around to see if anyone was looking from any unexpected location. As much as I had come to accept my reality, these "coming home" moments always reminded me of the difficulty of my new life. My father carried me out of the car and into the house, where he laid me on the same bed that I used to sleep on before I left. The bed faced the front door, so I had a front-row view to look straight 'outta' road. Also, I had a window to my right. It was almost like déjà vu. The only difference was, my entire life had changed, and from now, it would always be different.

Old Friends and Old Habits

Granny's husband built the house we lived in, and he was there when I went home. He was so delighted to see me, and just when I thought that no one else saw me when I arrived, oh boy, was I wrong. You see, in the country, we all look out for each other. Neighbors always gave an eye out over each other's property, whether you're there or not. So, soon enough, some of the neighbors were already coming over, and when they saw me, they were glad but also sad. Some of them said, "Bwoy, Kevin, this is not the way you left here. But is suh we get you back, so we still giving thanks you have life."

Others said, "when you got shot, you could have died. God saved your life and gave you another chance, mi bwoy."

Eventually, the news of my return home spread like wildfire. The famous line became, "Guess who come and down a granny? Nuh Battu Reds."

"Battu Reds" was my alias in the community of Sevens Heights. As the days went by, my friends visited me and 'boom off' my fist. Greeting me, they said, "What a gwaan youth, you good mon?"

Naturally, some of them were sad when they saw me and said, "bwoy Battu, if you never leave and go to town, none of this would have happened to you. The whole of us would still be here running up and down together like always."

At that moment, I started to think, "Probably dem is right. What if I never did leave, might be none of this would have happened." But guess what? It had already happened, and there was nothing we could do to change that. We just had to accept it and live with it because one cannot undo the past in life. We can attempt to fix it in some cases, but there is no fixing for other situations. Things happen, and destiny seals our fates.

Meet me by the River

Regardless of those issues, it was a good feeling to see my friends again. I was back on my home turf, where I spent most of my childhood days running up and down and going to the river. I wasn't a good swimmer; all my other friends were much better swimmers than I was. It was like they were a school of fish in the river. On one of those trips to the river, I had a near-drowning experience. One of my friends volunteered to bring me across a deep section of the river on his back. You know, boys. Boys will always be boys, they say, and so I decided to go with him. I climbed onto his back, and we started our journey.

While we were going across, I don't know what happened, but I fell off his back and quickly started to sink. Back then, I thought that was it for me. I didn't anticipate the future near-death confrontation between myself and the gun in 1998. I couldn't predict the future. But alas, I was not to die by drowning. One of my other friends dived into the water and quickly pulled me out. I coughed until I felt like I was going to throw up because I had swallowed a bit of water as I struggled earlier. All was well the ended well that day. It is ironic how death seemed to have been after me, but I stayed away from deep waters since that day.

Friends Like Mine

Every day my friends came to visit me. Those who worked would come and give me a link when they returned home in the evenings. Others knew granny and her husband, and they also came to visit me. Once they became familiar with the fun-loving person I was, everyone fell in love with Kevin. Every day we chatted about a variety of stuff and read the bible together. We laughed, ran jokes, and reminisced on the good old days. I am an old soul. Sometimes the jokes would be so intense, we laughed until our eyes watered, and tears ran down our cheeks. Our glee and laughter often resulted in stitches in our bellies. Sometimes, my visitors would fall to the ground, wrapped in a ball of laughter, and roll from left to right like a donkey on his back.

We challenged each other with many riddles, some of which had our brains under tremendous pressure for hours to get them right. When it came to telling jokes, riddles, and duppy stories, country people stand out. We are the best at what we do! Incredibly hilarious was the duppy story about the calf with fire coming out of his eyes, drawing behind him the big, long chain wrapped around his neck. This was a terrifying image in my young mind at the time. Some of the stories were so scary. When the kerosene oil lamp was turned down to its lowest in the nights, you were forced to lay there in the dark and ponder the stories until the gracious hands of sleep finally came for you.

There were two sisters who I came to know in that season of my life, and we became fast friends. They never left me out. They were very nice girls, especially the younger of the two. As soon as the morning light, she came over to my house, and we would play all day. We also ate, drank, and played the snake game on my Nokia 3310 phone. We used to get the phone charged by a neighbor who used a car battery to run their TV. We also used another neighbor's Delco for charging because, at that time, the community did not have any electricity. We either used a kerosene oil lamp or a bottle torch to give light at night. We couldn't watch TV. The next best thing was the ability to listen to a small battery-powered radio where we kept up to date with news. We would play some games in a book just to pass the time and have fun. Sometimes, we would be up until late in the night, around nine or ten o'clock, before my friend would leave and go over to her house. Those were the days.

I am grateful for the friendships I've been a part of in this life. Many friends come to take from us, with nothing to return…but my friends gave of themselves in that season of my life, and I will forever remember that yes, those were indeed the days.

Chapter 8

Life Interrupted

With no electricity, the days and nights were mainly peaceful and quiet, especially the nights. You could hear a pin drop. You could see lots of fireflies, or peeney wallies as we called them, twinkling their lights everywhere. When it was moonshine in the country, the view was fantastic and truly spectacular. People sat under trees or at their doorways and chatted until the late hours of the night. I think life in the country is the best. There is something about the country breeze that is always cool. It always smells fresh when it hits you; it feels like it was coming off the dew from a misty mountain. It is clean, light, and uncorrupted by the dirt of the towns.

On Sundays, granny went to church some distance away from home. Her deacon took her on his motorbike when his wife wasn't going, or she traveled via public transportation. Granny's husband and I remained at home, and he cooked dinner. He wasn't as good a cook as my granny, but he did his thing. He was a single amputee. He had only one foot. Everyone who knew him called him either Mr. Brown or Brother Brown. He was a great musician, a multi-talented, very active jack-of-all-trades, and master of many. He played several musical instruments. He told me that an angel taught him to play music in a dream. He also said that he was the leader of a band called the Blue Glade Mento band when he was younger.

Mr. Brown was also an ex-policeman. I remember one of many stories he shared with me. One day, he left his home and was walking on the road when he met a tall, muscular man who asked him for money to buy something to eat. Mr. Brown said he didn't have any cash on him, but he wasn't far from his house. So, he turned back with the man and headed to his home. Upon his arrival, he told his mother to give the man something to eat. The man sat on the lower part of the verandah step, and Mr. Brown stood behind him. But he said that while the man was there eating, he observed this man closely and noticed how shabbily dressed he was. He decided to go back to his room, where he changed his clothes because he was wearing plain clothes. He exchanged the comfort of these clothing for the formality of his police uniform. He took up his government-issued gun, a revolver, and put it into his pocket. He went and stood right where he was before returning to his room, directly behind the man. Mr. Brown said that the man was so frightened when he finished eating, turned around and saw him. The man was shocked when he saw my granny's husband, the same man who brought him home, gave him something to eat, now dressed in formal attire.

Mr. Brown told the man, "Come, we are going up to the police station."

The man was quite resistant and said firmly, "I am not going anywhere with you."

Now Mr. Brown was small in stature and very slim. This man was big and thick but, he said insistently to the strange man, "If you do not come, I will shoot you in your foot."

Finally, the man complied. Mr. Brown caused the man to walk in front of him. The two of them walked all the way to the station because vehicles weren't so popular in those days. He said that when he stepped into the police station with the man, his colleagues were surprised. When they ran some checks, the man was wanted by the police for several break-ins and numerous other crimes. Even the clothes that this man was wearing were stolen. Apparently, the man had jumped a fence into someone's yard and stole their clothes. Mr. Brown brought a criminal to justice through his act of bravery and smartness.

Even though he had only one foot, it was amazing to see Mr. Brown climb trees. He was very active on his one foot. We raised many goats, and he was the one who took care of them. He tied some of them, and the rest of them he allowed to run free, especially when they went out to feed in the morning. When they returned in the evening, they would drink water and go straight into the pen.

Sometimes, when he carried the ones he tied out, they would run around him, entangling him in the ropes. This caused him to fall to the ground and bruise his hands and foot. I felt so sorry for him, and it hurt me so much to know that I couldn't get up to help him in any way.

I felt so bad within myself because of all the struggles he had to endure to take care of his goats while thieves watched and stole them. One night, granny and one of my uncles, her son, went to a nine-night or dead yard at York Town. Mr. Brown and I were at home that night. He locked all the goats in their pen. Still, there was one goat that Mr. Brown didn't put in the pen. He tied him in an empty fowl coup instead. Perhaps he was on to something because the following day, when we woke up and opened the door, all the goats in the pen were gone. Thieves came during the night while we slept and took every one of the goats, except the one in the fowl coup. They did not know that it was there.

The pen was now empty. The thieves took everything. I couldn't believe that people could be so heartless. They stole from an old one footman and an old woman with her disabled grandson, who laid on his belly night and day. All we did was try to raise some goats. They took all but one of the goats. Despite what greeted us that morning, we didn't cry. We didn't panic either. I just took up my little Nokia phone, called my uncle, went to the 'nine-night' with her, and told him to tell granny that thieves stole all the goats, only leaving one. He said that when he told her, she cried.

He told me that he turned towards her and said, "Mama, don't cry," and she dried her tears. They said that when they left out for the 'nine-night,' the previous night, they passed a strange van parked nearby in the community and that the men in the van even greeted them. Unfortunately, no one knew the vehicle, nor the men in it, and the loss of our goats was the price we had to pay.

Granny was old, so she could not work anymore. Her husband was also old and was disabled, so he could not work either. Raising their goats was their primary means of income. This was their bread and butter. The robbery was a massive blow to them, but it would not keep them down forever.

The single goat that the thieves left behind began to reproduce over time or, as we say in Jamaica, have kids. Her kids grew quickly, and they too started to have kids. The herd was growing nicely until one morning when we woke up. Lightning struck twice in the same place. This time, the thieves did not even leave a single goat behind when they came. They left us with nothing. The only other source of income for granny was her little pension, and I mean little because it wasn't much. Her husband was not a pensioner, although he was an ex-police officer. I mentioned earlier that he was very talented. So, it shouldn't be surprising when I say that

Mr. Brown could also earn by building furniture. He was an excellent furniture maker, one of the best. Whenever Mr. Brown made a piece of furniture, he took his time; he didn't rush. He would cut every piece of wood so neatly; it fit in place perfectly. It was as if he were making them to last for a lifetime. As a result of this, everyone was pleased when they gave him a job.

Let there be Light!

As time passed, the residents of Sevens Heights came together and moved towards obtaining electricity for the area. Everyone signed up the necessary documents. Someone delivered the paperwork and monies to the Jamaica Public Service's (J.P.S.) office. Soon, the contractors came to the community and started to 'string' the houses. When we saw this, the level of excitement was high! Why shouldn't it be? If electricity finally arrived in Sevens Heights, it would be a historical sight. A ray of hope! A beacon of light. It had long been like dark ages or even a wilderness for decades. Every day, the guys came and worked very hard to see how quickly they could finish. Until one day, finally, they completed the 'stringing' of the houses.

Simultaneously, J.P.S. was putting up their posts in the area. Everyone now had their post put up in their yard with the J.P.S. meter attached. Eventually, J.P.S. came to check the houses and, thankfully, passed them all. And now for the big moment! Oh, how the anticipation was killing us.

"Get on with it!" I thought. And then it happened. Light in Sevens Heights at last! Finally, after so many years, the darkness was lifted. It was like a long walk to freedom. Now, the residents could switch on lights in their homes and their yards. People could watch their televisions and have some cool ice water and juice to drink. It was like living in Kingston again. Granny bought a television to celebrate the moment. I am sure it was a sacrifice, but it was a feel-good moment for everyone.

Hurricane Season

The house we lived in was a board structure. It was solid. Granny's husband built this house. It had passed through many intense hurricanes over the years, even wild hurricane Gilbert, and it still stood firm. Unfortunately, as time passed, termites ate away at the wooden structure, the sides, the top, just about everywhere.

One year, a hurricane, I think it was hurricane Ivan, threatened Jamaica. We were hoping and praying that it wouldn't hit our country. When nightfall approached, the dreaded monster made landfall, setting its deadly feet onto Jamaican shores. Hurricane Ivan unleashed its onslaught of furious winds and heavy rains. It was powerful. I was lying on my bed, and all the windows and doors were tightly shut. Suddenly, the roof on my side of the house started to lift, moving up and down. It was like someone was juggling a football. I was there joking about it, but soon, things changed. My brother, who was with us at the time, came and held me by my feet, and I walked off the bed on my two hands and ran on them straight into the other room. We lived in a two-bedroom house at the time. For the remainder of that night, I laid flat on my belly on the water-filled floor, with the rain blowing heavily into the house. I was soaked from head to toe. I had to push my head under a dresser draw. We didn't get any sleep that night. It was the longest night of my life.

The Aftershocks

When the morning finally came, we looked into my room, and we were looking outside. It was as if someone used a crowbar and pulled apart the whole thing. The top, side, and back were gone. Despite everything, we were thankful. God was good to us because right beside the room we were in throughout the night, a huge tree fell alongside the house. The tree could have killed us if it had fallen on top of the house. This was not to be. Mercy was on our side.

Two or three friends passed by the house that same morning, and they could see that part of the house had blown down. They came and used some zinc to insert into the roof area where the water was blowing in. They were also checking in on us to see if we were okay otherwise. That morning, my skin was so white from the rain beating against my skin all night. But we survived.

As the days passed, I saw that staying on granny's side of the room was comfortable. I stayed there for a few weeks until they could fix my side of the room to allow me to move back over. When that happened, it was a relief because I liked my own space. Back on my side, I could get to look out through my windows and my door again.

Chapter 9

Granny to the Rescue

Granny has an older sister by her mother's side. Her name is Esther. One day, granny went to the market, and someone saw her and said, "Miss Ruby, you don't know what? Your sister is in the poor house."

Granny said, "What? How did she get there?"

She could not believe what her ears were hearing. When she came home from the market, she told her husband, Mr. Brown, "Someone told me that my sister is in the poor house."

He said in surprise, "What? How did that happen?" She responded in her usual calm tone, "I hear is who brought her there, but I am going to take her out."

Her husband said to her, "It is your sister. Go for her".

So, Granny went to verify whether what she heard was true and when she got there, she realized it was so. She cried when the reality of her sister's situation hit her. She returned home, and with tears in her eyes, she told us that her sister was there as reported.

Later that week, she hired a taxi and went for her sister. It happened so quickly. When the cab returned and stopped at our gate, her sister could hardly walk; they had to lift her out. She and I were staying in the same room, but she stayed on another bed. My grandaunt was quite slim until granny started taking care of her. She quickly gained weight from the cornmeal porridge, oats porridge, banana and plantain porridge with peanut, and cowskin soup with beans she frequently ate. Granny was the one who had to feed her because she couldn't feed herself.

Granny also had to bathe her, comb her hair, and change her clothes. Granny did almost everything for her. As some would say, her head would also "go and come" because she was somewhat senile. The scars of age were visible in her life. She would often talk to herself or say things that weren't real. Sometimes, granny would give her something to drink, and this calmed her mind down. When she was okay, she was a lot of fun to be around. She told many stories and gave plenty of jokes. You would often laugh yourself to tears, and when you look at her, you could see the difference that being with us made.

Before you know it, she was putting on weight and gaining strength. She could soon walk around on her own with a piece of stick. She walked to the toilet and went outside to sit down under a tree to get some fresh air. People in the community were amazed to see the difference since granny had taken her in. People were saying, "Miss Ruby, God has a blessing in heaven for you. Keep up the good work."

I, too, was amazed. Granny had me who was crippled, her husband with one foot, and now her sister, who was over 90 years old and in need of care. Yet, she was taking care of the three of us all at once. What a blessed and strong woman she was. Notably, she never complained. She was always humble.

The Cock Named Jack

My father, who was back in Kingston, had a roaster. He said that the roaster was "bad" because of his behavior. Often, the roaster would go hungry if my father was not there to feed him. No one in the yard would deal with him because of his bad attitude. My father said there used to be many other fowls in the yard, but dogs came and ate them. However, the dogs couldn't beat the roaster. It was always a bitter battle between the dogs and that roaster, but he always won. Granny, who is my father's mother, raised many fowls. So, he said that he was going to give her the roaster. My father said that he had to use a sheet and throw it over the roaster when he wanted to catch him. That was the only way he could lay hands on him and tie him up to ship him to granny's house.

When my father brought him to the country, Mr. Brown took charge of him and gave him a name. He called him Jack. Mr. Brown was the only one who could come and take Jack up in his arms without receiving a peck. Only Mr. Brown alone could go beside him. I don't know how he did it. One day, Granny and her husband were not home. It was just me, one of my friends, and Aunt Esther. Shortly after Aunt Esther went outside to use the toilet, I heard a voice calling for my friend. I said to him, "Hear Aunt Esther calling you."

He went outside, and he later told me that when he saw Aunt Esther, she was involved in a fight with the roaster. I don't know how Jack managed to get away because he was always tied under the cherry tree. Apparently, Aunt Esther was the first thing in its sight when he escaped. He was attacking her, running after the poor lady, and pecking on her behind. It was a good thing my friend was there to run to her rescue. He was a vicious and violent fowl.

Unfortunately, Jack soon fathered some other roasters, sons if you would, who were almost as violent as him. Some of you may know the proverbs which say, 'like father, like son' and 'blood follow vain.' Often, I could hear granny outside fighting with the roasters. Sometimes, she had to knock them down flat.

One day, one of my uncles, Miss Ruby's son, came to look for us. He didn't know about Jack's bad attitude, and he went and stood beside him under the cherry tree. When Jack saw that my uncle was in range, he ran and pecked him right through his socks. My uncle was stunned but not seriously hurt.

No one could walk in the yard in peace. Eventually, we realized that we couldn't keep those roasters for long. They were now on the most wanted eating list because of their bad behavior and vicious assaults. They left us with no other choice but to take them out. Granny did the hard work, and she cooked them with love. Their meat was rich, simply delicious! My uncle even ate some of Jack's boys, perhaps as revenge for the pecks he received from their father. Indeed, 'badness' doesn't pay, but they learned this the hard way. They may have lived a little longer but for their bad behavior.

The Choices We Make

Aunt Esther's daughter eventually heard that Granny went for her mother and had her at our home taking care of her. Granny's niece indicated that she wanted her mother back in her care. Of course, one wonders, but the daughter insisted that this was her mother. One day, she indicated that she wanted her mother to come and spend a few weeks with her. So, Granny told Aunt Esther, "Your daughter said that she wants you to come and spend a couple of weeks with her." Surprisingly, she said yes, she wanted to go just for a couple of weeks.

Granny said, "Well, it is your daughter."

So, they packed some of her stuff together, and she went. That left me, Granny, and her husband, Mr. Brown, alone at home. The original trio.

Chapter 10

New Home and New Troubles

I have this cousin, another of granny's grandsons. We grew up in the country at the same house together for a short while before he left and went to Kingston to live. He would often come back and look for us. On one occasion, my cousin went overseas for some time, and he decided to build a house on granny's land for himself, for her, her husband, and I would also get a room. Mr. Brown was the one overseeing the construction of the house. Eventually, the money came from overseas, and we bought the materials. Day by day, the workmen would come in and the work. They dug the foundation, and the construction was well on its way.

One day, Mr. Brown and I were alone at home when he began to cough. When he spat, he coughed up blood, and when I saw it, I knew that this couldn't be good. When granny came in the evening, he told her, and she let me call his brother. He was updated about his brother's situation. The brother arrived in the morning, and granny readied Mr. Brown for his trip to the doctor. As Mr. Brown left the house, you could see a grim look in his eyes as he held his head straight, without looking behind him once. He went and sat in the car with a sad look on his face. I realized that Mr. Brown must have been thinking, deep down inside, that something was wrong with him. He was correct. When they brought him to his doctor, the doctor sent him straight to the hospital after the examination. When he went there, they admitted him because, as it turned out, Mr. Brown was diagnosed with the disease that everyone fears, the monster. That monster is called cancer.

It had already eaten away inside his stomach and was on its way up to his head. For almost all his life, he has been a hard smoker. He would smoke a lot of cigarettes and weed, Ganja. He wasn't a big eater either. Often, he would smoke more than he ate. Sometimes, granny would quarrel with him just to get him to stop smoking and eat food.

He was in the hospital for about a week. Then one night, I heard my phone ring. I picked it up and looked at it. It was a number I did not know. I answered, "Hello." A woman's voice greeted me on the line. She said that she was calling from the hospital to inform me that Mr. Brown had died. When she said "died," instantly tears began to stream down my face. I felt like a shock wave had passed through my body. I paused, lost for a moment. I forgot that the lady was still on the phone until she said, "Hello?" and I said okay and hung up the phone.

Granny was in her room, but she heard me talking on the phone, so she jumped up and said, "Kevin, is what?"

I delivered the news as best as I could. I said, "It is the hospital that called. Mr. Brown is dead."

Seconds later, she opened the front door and ran outside. She lifted her voice to the heavens and wept loudly. She cried for him. I also cried for this man, who loved me well, even though we were not blood. He used to do so much for me, even with only one foot. He would empty my pail and empty my urine bottle. When granny went out, he used to cook for me. If I needed something at the shop, he went and bought it for me. I just couldn't believe that he was dead.

He died at age 76. A great man was gone forever, but his memory will live on because of the good he had done. Despite his limitations, he did so much. It made me pause, and I thought about life. It is but only for a short time. Mr. Brown was like the hero who we would never forget and the legend that never dies. He was both in one.

I had to deliver the bad news to others as well, and so I called his brother and told him, "Your brother has died. He is gone."

In the morning, I called Mr. Brown's two sons, who were overseas, and informed them of their father's death. I called up the rest of the family members and let them know of his passing. By this, granny told the neighbors, and word started to circulate about his death. People came by to pay their condolences because he was a very well-respected man in the community. Inside and out, people were coming, and many helped cut the yard, clean up, put up tarps, and set up domino tables. The dead yard was unofficially happening. People visited every night to play dominoes, laugh and talk and set up with us.

The church that granny attended most of her life refused to host the funeral service for her husband. Granny had set the funeral date for a Sunday because most people who wanted to attend the funeral could only make it on a Sunday. But her pastor refused. He said that Mr. Brown wasn't a member of the church, and for that reason, a Sunday funeral service could not be held for him there. Of course, that did not sit well with the rest of the family. They said granny attended the church for so long, and now that her husband died, the pastor refused to host the funeral service for him on a Sunday. They were really cut up about it, quite angry, and rightly so, amid their pain.

The family considered where to find a church willing to host the funeral service for Mr. Brown. Another female Pastor, our neighbor, called her Bishop and asked if he could hold the service. He didn't hesitate or think twice; he said yes. He didn't even know Mr. Brown or granny. He never saw them before, but he agreed to host the funeral service and bury Mr. Brown on a Sunday. We could continue with our plans.

Mr. Brown's two sons didn't get to come to his funeral. My cousin, who was overseas and helping us build the house, came out, along with his sister, who was in the States. They came together. The funeral date was set, and they got straight to business. They shopped, purchasing a large portion of items, and spending a load of money.

The big night came, the nine-night, which was also the final night before the funeral, where people came together to eat and drink. Speaking of eating and drinking, there was plenty of food to go around. There was liquor, curried goat, fish, chicken, rum, Guinness, Heineken, beer, and soup. There was a band playing, and people were singing and dancing straight through until morning. It was nice. People came from all over, near and far. It was the first time I ever stayed up all night without sleep. The nine-night was one to talk about; it 'shot' as we say here in Jamaica. The family went all out. It ended in the morning, and people left to get ready for the funeral.

While everyone was busy getting ready to go, I wasn't. I started to think of Mr. Brown, and I just couldn't bring myself to look at his lifeless body. It was too much for me to take. Everyone else went, but I couldn't go.

I heard about it later that day. What a service it turned out to be. All the church brethren supported it. It was a grand send-off for Mr. Vincent Neville Brown. While I was alone at home, I thought about how I should have been there. Maybe he would have wanted me to be there. To tell you the truth, I lamented that decision not to go.

It has left a weight on my shoulders that I must carry for the rest of my life.

When everyone came home later that day, they told me how big and nice the funeral was. I wasn't surprised; Mr. Brown was well known. Many people went to pay their last respects to him. After the funeral, they feasted again. Those who were to go home left, and those that could stay, remained for a while.

The following Sunday, granny went to her home church and informed them that she would no longer be a member of that church anymore. She left after that. She became a member of the church that buried her husband. The members of that church grew to love her a lot and called her Mother Brown.

The cousin who lived overseas, who was building the house, stayed for about a month. He got to see some work done on the house for the first time. When he came, he saw that I was staying on an old iron bed. The irons were rusty because we had that bed for many years. We grew up sleeping on it. He decided to get me a little divan bed, and he also gave me my first phone. He gave me money which I used to buy my first Gameboy advance. Many other people also got phones, watches, clothes, shoes, and money.

Every day for that month, they cooked a big pot of food or "run a boat," as we say here in Jamaica, and drank a lot of liquor. But you all know what they say that all good things must come to an end. It was time for my cousin to leave, so he went back to America. The work on the house continued despite his departure. It was going on well until gunmen murdered the contractor who was building the house. He had a little truck that he used to carry and sell water in the community. One morning, he went to catch water. When his family saw that it was getting late, and he didn't return home, they went in search of him and found him dead. He was shot in the head. The building project paused for a while, but it was near completion as the roof was finished. It would be some time before things picked up again. But life continued, this time around, without Mr. Brown.

The Vision

One day, granny went to the market. When she returned home, she said to me, "Kevin, I saw Sister Girly at May Pen today, and she said she got a message for you."

Sister Girly was one of granny's church sisters and a spiritual lady. Upon hearing this, I started to wonder what I did. I couldn't walk, so I was always in one place. I know I didn't do anything wrong. In my time, when you know spiritual people, who say that they got a message for you, you know that you needed to start self-examination. But, a couple of days went by, and finally, she came to see me. Her son drove her because she was a big lady. She walked with a cane, little by little, into the yard until she reached the front door, my front door. She stepped inside the house and sat down on a chair. She greeted us and began to sing. We had a short prayer service.

Then she said, "Kevin, I get a vision from the Lord to come to you. And the vision is to do something to you and to give you two Psalms."

She carried out the instructions she got from her vision, and then she gave me the two psalms. One of the psalms spoke of difficult times ahead that I would face, and the other said that I should rejoice in the Lord and continue to trust in him. A few people were there as witnesses. When she finished, she left.

Chapter 11

Death Came Knocking ... Again

G ranny had church services twice per week: Wednesdays and Sundays. There was this man who, Mr. Brown, when he was alive, had done some good for him. But when he wanted to pay Mr. Brown, my step-grandfather didn't charge him. That man carried granny to church every day that she went. Whenever he couldn't pick her up, he would send a taxi to take her. One Wednesday, granny woke up, looked about breakfast, and gave me something as usual. Then she got ready to go to church. The car came, and it was time for her to leave. She said, "Take care, Kevin." I said, "Yes, granny. You too."

When she left, I was alone at home until two of my friends came by. One of my friends, Blacka, worked but got his day off on Wednesdays. He would come and borrow my PSP game because I had FIFA on it. He loved to play FIFA like me. So, I would always have it charged for lending Blacka on those days. When he came that Wednesday, hours passed before he had to leave and collect some basic school children that lived in his yard. So, Blacka went and said that he would soon be back.

I then gave my other friend fifty dollars and told him to buy some weed for me. When he returned, I sent him to dig a plant nearby, which I will not name. When he came back with the plant, I told him to wash it, put the weed and the plant into a pot, and boil them. When he finished boiling them, he threw the liquid into a container and brought it to me. He then said that he had to leave, which he did. Then I took the boiled herbs and poured them into a juice bottle. I had another liquid in a little bottle. When boiling roots, people would pour some in it. So, I poured some of that liquid into the liquid that my friend boiled.

When I poured the liquid into the juice bottle, I instantly noticed that the color changed from a light grey to an almost transparent watery clear appearance. I placed the bottle on a stool to my right and resumed playing some FIFA. I loved football. I had one eye on the game and the other on the bottle with the liquid. My mind could not rest because I was curious about why the color changed. At the same time, I heard a small voice inside my head saying to me, "Kevin, don't drink it." I listened to this voice inside my head as it kept on repeating, over and over, "Don't drink it. Don't drink it," like an alarm clock. All this time, I was alone.

For some reason, out of curiosity, I put down the game and took up the bottle. I poured a little in the cover. I held the lid with my right hand and then lifted my hand towards my mouth, stuck out my tongue, and tipped a little of the liquid on my tongue. I didn't drink any because I still heard the voice inside my head that kept telling me not to drink it. When I tipped the little on my tongue, I covered the bottle and put it back on the stool. I picked up the game and continued to play. About 3 to 4 minutes after, I began to feel weak. It felt like my body was shutting down. No wonder they say curiosity killed the cat, I thought as I became weaker by the second. I was no cat. This was me, a man. My strength was failing fast. I could no longer raise myself with my hands. I had to lie down flat on my stomach. My heart was beating fast, racing like a race car on a track. It felt like my heart was going to explode in my chest. I could feel my lips getting dry and weariness in my eyes. My brown complexion turned dark.

By this, Blacka had returned after collecting the children from basic school. He came through the gate and stepped on the verandah. As he walked into my room, he saw me, almost motionless, on the bed. He asked, "What is wrong with you?"

I replied, "I don't feel so good."

Again, he asked, "What is wrong with you?"

I again said, "I don't feel good." I barely mumbled the words out of my mouth. All this time, granny was at church. I managed to reach out my left hand on the bed, picked up my phone, went into contacts, and scrolled until I found granny's family doctor's number. I dialed it and called him. The phone rang, and I waited. After about the third ring, he answered, "Hello."

I said, "Good afternoon, Doc. My name is Kevin Robinson, and I am Miss Brown's grandson. She is at church. I am at home alone, and I am not feeling well." I didn't explain the details to him.

I didn't have any money, but I was going to see him. His office was in May Pen, Clarendon. I lived in Clarendon, near May Pen. All this time, Blacka stood there as if he was in a state of panic. I then called another friend of mine, Bigga. I knew that he wasn't supposed to be home that day because he was going to class and only came home on weekends. Luckily for me, he was home when I dialed his number. He answered, and I said, "Poppie," - that was the name I called him - "I don't feel so good."

He asked, "What's wrong?"

I said, "I don't feel good." By the time I said, "I don't feel good," the second time and looked out of my window, I saw him running towards my house. He ran straight into my room and lifted me off the bed in my shorts and shirt. He took me out to the road. At the same time, a taxi was coming, and he stopped it. Blacka opened the door, and Bigga put me inside, and then he entered. He told Blacka to lock up the house.

As the taxi drove off, I told him that I called Doctor Brown. While on the way, I could feel myself sleeping away. At times, I slipped in and out of consciousness. Bigga had to keep talking to me to keep me awake. Finally, the taxi arrived at the office in May Pen. Bigga lifted me from the car and brought me into the doctor's office immediately. He placed me on a little bed in the office, and the doctor came over and began to examine me straightaway. He asked me what happened and if I drank anything. I don't recall if I answered, but as he questioned me, he kept on shining his little light into my eyes. He told me to stick out my tongue and to stretch out my left hand. I obeyed as best as possible in the circumstances.

He took a piece of cotton, wet it with an unknown liquid, and wiped off my skin so he could see my veins. He then inserted a needle into the vein and attached a drip with a solution to it. I then told the doctor that I had boiled some weed with another bush and added some roots. I told him I had noticed that the liquid changed color, so instead of drinking it, I tipped some on my tongue. Immediately, he wrote a letter, handed it to me, and sent me off to the hospital.

As it turned out, the mixture of the weed and the other bush with the roots had turned into a deadly poison. If I had consumed even a spoonful, I would have certainly died. When I gave Bigga the letter, he went out quickly in search of a taxi. The one that brought us only dropped us off and left. He didn't get paid, and neither did the doctor. Before you knew it, Bigga came back to me in a taxi, and off we went to the hospital. The sun was so hot, and the traffic seemed noisier than usual with the blowing of horns and loud music everywhere. Perhaps it was how I was feeling, but everything was so confusing.

I was uncomfortable. My back felt stiff, and I couldn't wait to lay down somewhere. Sitting up for so long was unbearable. I had a feeling that I couldn't quite explain. At last, the taxi arrived at the hospital. The security guard raised the bar that stretched across the entrance so that we could enter. When we came to a stop, Bigga went to look for a wheelchair. When he found one, he came back for me, and once I was seated, Bigga pushed me to the hospital's administrative section, where he gave them the letter that Doctor Brown wrote. They read it and then completed my registration process. We waited for some time. Evening came, and nightfall was following closely behind.

I had a few granny's church brethren's phone numbers, so I told Bigga to call one of the numbers and ask them to inform granny of my trip to the hospital.

Shortly after that, I said to Bigga, "I don't feel so good,"

He responded, "I know, but just try and keep up."

I said weakly, "I feel like am going to vomit."

He said, "Let me go check to see if I get something that you can vomit in." Bigga went in search of something, but it is too late. By the time he came back, I had spilled everything on the floor and my clothes. My stomach content looked extremely green, but in the aftermath, I said to him, "Bigga, I am so uncomfortable. I can't sit up any longer. My back is killing me. Just put me on the floor to lie down."

He responded, "You can't lie on the floor."

I begged, "Please, Bigga, please." But he insisted, "I can't do that. Just try and hold on."

He left me to check on what was preventing them or delaying them from admitting me to the ward or addressing my condition. After a while, he returned and said all the beds were full, so I had to wait.

Granny came at last. She found us, and I told her what I had done earlier that day. We waited the whole night into the other morning before a bed finally became available. I was brought on to the ward and put in a bed. I laid flat on my belly. Oh my gosh, what a relief! My back felt like it did not belong to me. I yawned multiply times. I was tired, exhausted, really, and sleep was calling my name. By this time, Granny and Bigga had to leave because it was the early hours of the morning.

I had barely fallen asleep when a nurse came to take my blood pressure and checked my temperature. A porter soon followed and placed me into the wheelchair and brought me into a small room. I saw a woman who made me take off my shirt before the porter put me on a bed to lie on my back. She came over to me, took some wires connected to a machine, and taped them on my stomach. She went back to the device, where she monitored the screen for some time. I later found out that she checked my heart to see if the poison had damaged my heart. Thankfully, there was no damage. I knew this from the expression on her face, and it was a pleasant relief, a green light indicating that I was in the clear in that regard. My heart was all right.

After she finished running the test, I put on my shirt. The porter put me back in the wheelchair and took me back to my bed on the ward.

The doctor monitored and changed the drip as necessary. On one occasion, a nurse pushed a cart onto the ward and walked over to my bed. She stopped and spoke to me, "Stretch out your hand."

I stretched out my left hand, and she wrapped something around my arm, then used her finger to tap my vein. She reached for a needle and removed the cap. She bent forward and pushed the needle into my vein. I clenched my fist as I felt the sting of the needle breaking my flesh. I watched as she drew blood and pumped it into a small container. She drew some more as if the one bottle wasn't enough. She then pulled the strap from my arm and took a piece of cotton and put it over the sight from which she drew the blood. She taped the cotton down and left.

The blood the nurse drew from me was almost as dark as the hair on my head. I wasn't sure if that was good or bad. A Chinese doctor came to my bedside, assessed my condition, and spoke with me. He would be the doctor in charge of me for however long I would be there. I hope it wouldn't be an extended stay this time around.

Soon, it was breakfast time, and I got something to eat. Someone came and emptied my bedpan. One of the patients said to me, "There is blood in your bottle."

I looked down and checked my bottle. He was correct. I was passing blood in my urine, and I didn't even realize it. The doctors must have seen it, so I relaxed.

Throughout the day, cleaners came and mopped the floor, leaving the place smelling fresh and clean. Time had passed, and visiting hour came. Of course, Granny visited and brought some clothes for me. I was happy to see her, and I wished I could go home with her. The time of visitation passed quickly, and soon, Granny left.

I spent seven days in the hospital, and then finally, it was time for my discharge. The staff notified Granny, and soon enough, a taxi came to take me home. Nightfall arrived by the time I got home. I was relieved to finally be back home and in the warmth of my own bed.

Chapter 12

Aunt Esther's Last Song

Remember granny's sister, Aunt Esther? The same sister who granny rescued from the 'poor house' after hearing about her complicated situation? Shockingly, the daughter had asked for her mother after Granny took her in. I still have my opinions about why she came back for her mother, but I will allow you to draw your own conclusions here. Back then, she had said she wanted her mother to spend a couple of weeks with her, but the weeks turned into months, and eventually, the months turned into years.

Unfortunately, things did not go the way the daughter had expected them to work, as far as I am concerned, so the situation became a little tedious for Aunt Esther.

Even though Aunt Esther left her home, Granny would still travel to visit her. She was still her sister, her blood. Granny said that when she visited her sometimes, she was less than happy with the situation. Life was no bed of roses for Aunt Esther.

Granny eventually retained custody of her sister and brought her back home with the help of a hired taxi driver. This time, Granny had her for longer, and she tried her best to care for her sister.

One Friday morning, when we woke up, granny looked after both of us. She bathed us, made our beds, emptied our pails, and then gave us our breakfast. She then readied herself and went to the market, leaving Aunt Esther and me at home. We were good for the day.

In the evening, granny came home from the market and sat on her sister's bed. She asked her, "Sister, you want an orange?"

Aunt Esther replied, "Yes."

Granny stood up, went into the kitchen for a knife, and returned to sit on the bed. She peeled the orange, cut it into two halves, and then put the first piece at her sister's mouth. Aunt Esther tasted it and turned away her head with her eyes looking steadfast, straight into the rooftop. She did not blink once, and neither did a sound come from her mouth.

Granny started to panic and said to me with fear in her voice, "Kevin, is how sister look like she dead so?

"She a dead?" I asked in shock.

I didn't know how someone looked when they were dying. Granny ran out of the house and called one of her church brethren that lived nearby. I was there just looking at Aunt Esther on the bed, still shocked. When Granny and her church brethren were coming through the gate, I said to them in shock, "She is dead."

She wasn't moving. She slipped away peacefully at the age of 97. Granny started to cry, mourning the death of another loved one, this time her only sister. Thankfully, she had her church brethren who tried to comfort her.

She collected herself eventually, dressed, and headed off to the police station, where she reported her sister's death. The police later came with granny in a service vehicle, accompanied by another little van. When the police arrived, they stepped inside the house where Aunt Esther remained on the bed. One of the policemen asked some questions and checked her to verify that she was dead. The men that came in the little white van then came inside and wrapped up her body in a sheet. They placed her on a stretcher, put her into the van, and left for the funeral parlor.

After they left, I called one of her granddaughters and told her of her granny's death. She, in turn, called her granny's sons overseas and informed them of their mother's death. Some of her sons contacted us by phone.

Everything was planned, and before you knew it, a date was set for the funeral to take place. A few of granny's nephews were prepared for their mother's death because of her age. At nights, people stayed up with us, drank some rum, and played a little domino, the usual dead yard settings in Jamaica.

The day for the funeral drew closer. Some of her sons traveled from overseas, but some were unable to do so.

A small nine-night was held. It wasn't huge, but it was okay. The funeral was held the next day, which was a Saturday. Once more, I didn't go. I guess I'm not a big fan of funerals, after all.

It Takes a Village

So, with granny's husband and her sister gone, only granny and I were left in our little two-room board dwelling. We were comfortable and taking life as it came, one day at a time. Rain or shine, it was just the two of us.

Granny still went to church on Sundays. She would get up early in the mornings, fix my breakfast, and cook dinner before she left for church. Sometimes, I was home alone, but otherwise, some of my friends, or the two sisters I mentioned earlier, would stop by. Granny would tell the older sister that she was off to church now and so she should "take care of Kevin," and the sister always said, "Yes, granny."

She would come over and stay with me for some time and then returned home. After a while, she would come back to check and see if I was okay. She even brought dinner for me if granny wasn't coming home. On those nights, she slept over to keep me company. Otherwise, each time something had to be done or Granny needed a little helping hand, she would be ready to help. We had an excellent relationship.

Other neighbors would also come over, whether night or day, and we would chat and laugh. There was always someone stopping by, so I was never alone for too long. One of my friends, who had a keyboard and a guitar, carried one of the instruments with him when he visited. He would play, and I would sing. I believe I am an excellent composer. We would kick back and 'bill a vibe.' The neighbors' children would also set up old pans like a drum set and play. It was noise on top of noise at times. It was like we were keeping church. Most of us were raised in Christian homes, so it was in us. Sometimes we couldn't even hear ourselves think because of those old pans beating and echoing in our ears.

If you remember the man who Mr. brown helped in the past, he never left us out after Mr. Brown's death. Sometimes, he visited us two times per week or every Sunday, along with his girlfriend. We became very close, almost like family. Every time his car stopped at the gate, he and his girlfriend would shout out "Granny! Kevin!" as if our names were a sweet song.

Sometimes he called and asked what granny cooked. She told him what she cooked and asked if he wanted some. He would often respond, "Yes man, granny." He came for the food no matter how far he had to travel. He loved sweetsops, and for that, he would travel many hours and at any time.

A lady was living in Sevens Heights named Miss Maureen. One evening, she and a gentleman came to look for me. She said he was her boss, Mr. Kennett

Burrell. This was my first time seeing this man. He said goodnight, and I similarly replied. He then gave me a little package with some food items. He said he liked to visit people in my condition. He called us "shut-ins." We talked for a while; then, I shook his hand just before they left. He drove a white minivan. Since then, he came to see me every time he visited the area.

Unfinished but Habitable

My cousin, who was financing the construction of a home on Granny's land, got someone in the community to continue the building since the first contractor was killed. The house wasn't finished, but it was about 90% complete. Then, my cousin decided that he wanted Granny and I to move into the partially finished structure. So, we moved in. Granny got the back room, and I got the front room. It was a much closer view of the roadside as my bed faced the front window. It felt good. People passing on the road, whether walking or in a vehicle, would call out my name, "Kevin, (Batto Reds) what a gwaan youth? You good?".

Life was okay. It felt good to be alive. I woke up each morning and opened my window. I felt the fresh breeze blowing on my face and I enjoyed the smell of the fresh air and the sound of the singing birds. Hearing granny wake up and knowing that she was alive was a wonderful feeling. She often said, "Good morning, Kevin," and I replied, "Good morning, granny."

I'd say my prayers, brush my teeth, wash my face, and comb my hair while granny was in the kitchen fixing breakfast. I ate whatever she prepared. When I finished eating, I would call her for the plate, and she came and took the plates to the kitchen. I spent the rest of the day talking with friends who stopped by or playing games on my PSP.

Granny did everything for me. She washed, cooked, cleaned, and cut the yard. It was a large piece of land, our yard. She gave sections of the land to two persons so they could build houses and live. She is a blessed soul. I wish she could always remain active and well, but we know that nothing good lasts forever. She was getting older, not younger. This aspect of the future worried me then, and today, it still makes me anxious. She means the world to me. What would happen to me if she wasn't there? I was not excited to find this out. But life has a way of answering our unasked questions. Even so, I refuse to live a life without hope. I have been through too much to do that; in fact, life is much too precious to do that.

Chapter 13

The Land of the Living

With life-threatening gunshot wounds tattooed on my sixteen years old body by the hands of the adversary and a life without the use of my legs, what can I say in response to life's realities? I am grateful to be alive. That's my only response. I have woken up each morning since then, and I am thankful. Grateful. Yes, I am grateful to be in the land of the living.

I have seen many evils and heard many songs of sorrows. I was left to die, but you know what, I didn't. While the shots were being released from the chamber of that infamous gun, divine purpose was still on my life.

I believe God heard my cry from heaven and reached down that fateful day and grabbed me just in time from the silent arms of death. So, I do not doubt for a second that God gave me another chance to live, so I can be here today to tell you my story.

Despite your circumstances and what you're going through, never give up on life; I lost my mobility, and I didn't. Over the years, as time goes by and I look at my situation, I have learned to accept my reality. I don't want to live in denial because that's where we will lose the battle. So, as I wrap up this chapter of my story, I want to encourage someone going through something similar or even worse. Despite our circumstances, if you are reading this book, this minute, it means that, like me, you are still here in the land of the living. I still have a chance to make something of myself, which in my case, is a chance to turn my wounds into wisdom.

When one looks at me, one will see my limitations. However, despite my disabilities, I don't allow it to bar me from my daily activities because even though I am a legless man, I must move forward. I can't just sit around and feel sorry for myself, or the emotional wounds created by the physical wound on my body may never heal. I have a purpose beyond myself, and this pushes me forward. Granny now lives with me, and I with her. Since I was a 10-month-old baby, she took care of me, and as limited as I am now, I make it my duty to do all I can for my grandmother.

I make our breakfast in the mornings, get some other tasks sorted out as best as possible, and then make dinner for her when it's dinner time. Even with my disability, I am also a caretaker for my elderly grandmother.

I try to maintain our health as much as I can with what I have been given. I am forever grateful for the help my next-door neighbor offers to my grandmother and me. She comes over each day and takes care of my grandmother and I each day.

If I had a choice, I would not have chosen this experience for my life. Being bedridden for the past twenty years is no walk in the park. It's more like a walk-through hell. Yet, I walk through life with a story to tell, a lesson to share with every reader. We must make the best of what life hands to us. I have had people who have assisted me throughout my struggles, which has been one of my greatest motivators every day.

I don't intend to give up. Not now, not ever. It was Lance Armstrong who said quite wisely, "Pain is temporary. It may last a minute, or an hour, or a day, or a year, but eventually, it will subside, and something else will take its place. If I quit, however, it lasts forever." So, my journey continues by getting up every day, thanking God for another chance at life, and seeing the splendor of the world through my windows. I hope to finish the journey well. I hope my story will help you to live your story. In this life, people face unimaginable pain, both physical and emotional. I faced pain, real pain, true pain, and I survived; you too can survive.

Printed in Great Britain
by Amazon